The NatureTrail Book of
WILD ANIMALS

Rosemary Hartill

Identifying animals with this book

This book is about animals in Britain and Europe. It tells you how and where they live and when to see them. It also shows you the signs animals leave behind them and how to identify them. When you see something and you want to know what it is, use the book as follows:

Turn to the page in the book that deals with the kind of animal you have seen.
For example, pages 22-23 tell you about deer. If you can't see a picture of it there…

…turn to the section called **More mammals to spot** at the back of the book (pages 28-31). You may find a picture of it there.

Always make careful notes about the things you see, and try to identify them later.

First published in 1978 by
Usborne Publishing Ltd.,
20 Garrick Street
London WC2

Text and Artwork © 1978 by
Usborne Publishing Ltd.

Long-eared Bat

Stoat

Fox

Written by
Rosemary Hartill

Edited by
Jessica Datta

Consultant editor
Alfred Leutscher, B.Sc., F.Z.S.

With advice from
Iain Bishop, The Mammal Society,
and Daphne Hills

Designed by
Cloud Nine Design

Illustrated by
Graham Allen, Dave Ashby, John
Barber, Derick Bown, Christine
Howes, Robert Morton, Richard
Orr, Peter Stebbing and Annabel
Milne, David Wright

Printed in Belgium

Harvest Mouse

The NatureTrail Book of
WILD ANIMALS

About this book

This book is about European mammals. It tells you how they live, how and where to find them and shows you lots of clues and signs to look for.

Mammals are warm-blooded animals, which means that their body temperature does not vary much. Nearly all of them give birth to live young, who suckle milk from their mother. Most mammals are covered with hair or fur.

The book contains pictures of most of the common mammals you will see, so you can use it for identifying different species, or kinds, of mammals.

Contents

Roe Deer

How to start

Most mammals live in the country, but some, like certain kinds of rats and mice, live in towns. You can see mammals in different places— badgers live in woods, hares on farmland, otters on river banks and seals by the sea. Rabbits, squirrels and deer can be seen in town parks. Hedgehogs and foxes are common in and on the outskirts of towns.

Mammals are shy and frightened of people, so the best places to look for them are quiet, hidden spots like holes, ditches, trees and hedges. The animals' sharp senses will detect you unless you move slowly and quietly.

When to look
The best times to look for mammals are at dawn and dusk when many leave their homes to search for food. All mammals leave signs behind them—look for these at any time.

Spring and summer are good times to see mammals and their young. It is more difficult to see them in autumn and winter, but look for their food stores in autumn, and for tracks in the snow in winter.

Hat or hood

Knapsack for carrying food, plaster of Paris kit and plastic bags for collecting specimens.

Binoculars

Anorak or warm coat

Notebook and pencils

One or two pairs of socks

Wellingtons or strong shoes

Torch

What to wear

When you go out on a field trip to watch mammals, you will have to sit still for some time. Wrap up well. Wear dull coloured clothes so that you blend in with the background. Take something to eat, but don't pack food in paper bags that rustle. The noise would startle the animals.

If you want to watch mammals at night, use a torch with red cellophane over the beam. The red light will not disturb the animals.

Making notes

It is hard to remember everything you see, so make notes as you go along, marking down exactly where you find any specimens that you decide to take home or signs that you spot. Draw tracks carefully so that you can identify them later.

Torch to use at night

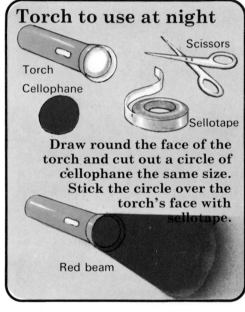

Torch

Cellophane

Scissors

Sellotape

Draw round the face of the torch and cut out a circle of cellophane the same size. Stick the circle over the torch's face with sellotape.

Red beam

What to look for

Tracks and runs

Look for mammal tracks in mud, sand or snow and after rain when the ground is soft. If you lose a trail, search in a circle around it (as shown above) until you find it again. Well-worn trails, or runs, may lead to a mammal's home.

Homes

Mammal homes can be on the ground, below it or above it. Piles of earth, dropped bedding or flattened vegetation are all signs that a home may be nearby.

Hair and droppings

Hairs are a good clue towards discovering which mammals live in a particular area. Look also at the size, shape, colour and position of droppings.

Meal remains

Look for half-eaten cones, nuts, vegetables and dead animals and birds. These may have tell-tale signs showing you which mammal has been eating them.

Damage

Many mammals damage trees and shrubs by feeding, rubbing or scratching. The position of these marks will help you to identify the mammal.

Making a map

Make a map like this one of an area near your house and mark on it the animals and animal signs that you see there. Some animals are more difficult to see than others, but you may find droppings and feeding signs to give you clues. Include paths, hedges, fences, streams and ponds on your map.

Over several months you can build up a picture of where animals live and hunt in your area. The picture below shows some of the animals you might spot. Red Squirrels are rare in Britain, but are more common in other parts of Europe.

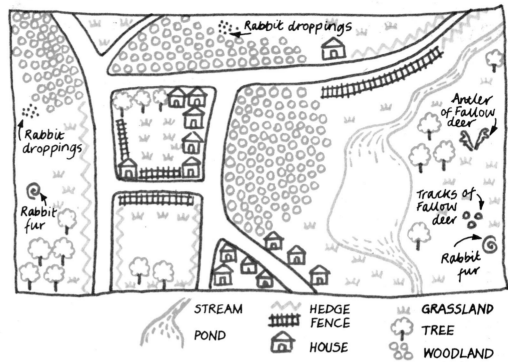

Rabbit droppings

Rabbit droppings

Rabbit fur

Antler of Fallow deer

Tracks of Fallow deer

Rabbit fur

STREAM	HEDGE FENCE	GRASSLAND
POND	HOUSE	TREE
		WOODLAND

Red Squirrel

Fallow Deer

Hedgehog

Rabbits

Wood Mouse

How to watch mammals

You need patience and some knowledge of a mammal's habits to catch more than a glimpse of it. Find out first where it lives, what it eats and when it is awake. Some small mammals are hard to find because they live underground. It is easier to watch larger mammals, but only when you have learnt to overcome their very good sense of smell. Be careful that the wind does not carry your scent to the mammal.

If you decide to build a hide, ask the landowner for permission before you start.

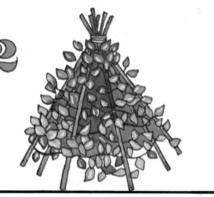

Stalking

SIT WELL ABOVE THE GROUND ON A BRANCH OR IN A HIDE SO THAT THE WIND CARRIES YOUR SCENT OVER THE MAMMAL'S HEAD

FIND A SPOT FACING THE WIND SO THAT THE MAMMALS CANNOT SMELL YOU. GET INTO POSITION EARLY

CHECK WIND DIRECTION WITH BITS OF GRASS OR A HANDKERCHIEF

Wigwam

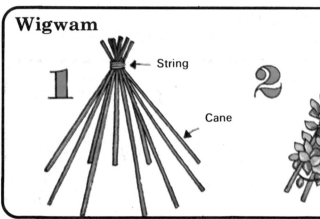

String

Cane

When you find a good place to see mammals, try building a simple hide to watch them from. Make a wigwam frame big enough to sit in from thin branches or bamboo

canes. Tie the tops together with string. Weave leafy twigs on to the canes. You may have to stay quietly inside for some hours, but it should be well worth the wait.

Tent

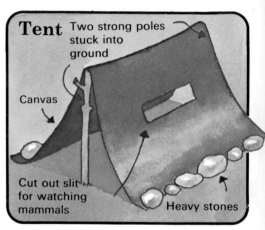

Two strong poles stuck into ground

Canvas

Cut out slit for watching mammals

Heavy stones

Make a simple tent using dull green or brown canvas or other heavy material. Hold the edges down with stones. Remember to wear dull-coloured clothes.

Tree platform

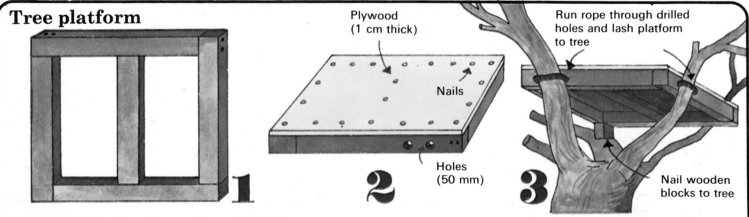

Plywood (1 cm thick)

Nails

Holes (50 mm)

Run rope through drilled holes and lash platform to tree

Nail wooden blocks to tree

1 Make a frame using pieces of wood 5 cm x 7.5 cm. Nail the joints together. The size and shape of the frame will depend on the tree.

2 Nail the platform floor to the frame. Drill pairs of holes where the frame will touch the branches.

3 Nail blocks to the tree to make the platform level. Tie the platform to the tree firmly. Make sure it is safe and secure before you use it.

Facing the wind

WHEN YOU SPOT A MAMMAL MOVE AROUND QUIETLY IN A WIDE CIRCLE UNTIL THE WIND IS BLOWING IN YOUR FACE. KEEP OUT OF SIGHT.

WHEN THERE IS NO COVER, CRAWL OR SLIDE NEARER TO THE MAMMAL ON YOUR STOMACH. FREEZE IF IT LOOKS UP

IF YOU ARE STALKING A DEER AND STILL CANNOT GET CLOSE ENOUGH, WAVE A WHITE HANDKERCHIEF ON A STICK. STAY HIDDEN. THE DEER MAY GET CURIOUS AND MOVE CLOSER

Baiting

Squirrels like nuts, raisins and chocolate

If you think you know where a mammal lives, try putting some food near its home. Hide and wait for the mammal to come out.

Stoats and Weasels like dead birds and mice, eggs and raw meat

To attract a Stoat or Weasel, put bait in some kind of tunnel (like a length of drainpipe) or in an arch made of stones.

Making plaster casts of tracks

If you find a good clear track, you can make a plaster cast of it.

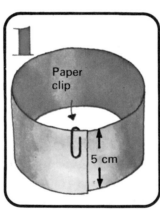

1 Paper clip

5 cm

Bend a strip of strong card (30 cm long) into a circle and join the ends together.

2

Remove leaves and bits of twig. Push the card ring into the ground.

3 Plastic spoon

Plastic bowl

Put some water in a bowl. Sprinkle plaster of Paris up to same level. Stir to a paste.

4

Pour the paste in the ring near the edge. Tap the ring to remove any air bubbles.

5

When set (20 minutes), lift up the cast with a knife. Gently remove the ring.

6 Paint

Clean the finished cast under a tap. You can paint it and give it a coat of clear varnish.

Badgers

Badgers are common in Britain, especially in hilly, wooded country. They are nocturnal animals, which means that they hunt, eat and play at night. During the day they rest in their underground homes, called setts. This is the best time to look for the sett entrance, using the clues shown on these pages. Go back to watch the Badgers come out in the evening, preferably taking an adult with you.

Badgers have poor eyesight, but their senses of smell and hearing are very sharp. You should get into position, facing the wind, about an hour before sunset so that your arrival doesn't frighten them. Wear warm, dark clothes and wait patiently.

Footprints in the sand

To check if a sett is being used, put some wet sand round the entrance and smooth it. Put down twigs too. Look next day for tracks and check to see if the twigs have been disturbed. When Badgers walk, the hind foot steps into the track left by the fore foot.

Look for hairs at the sett entrance. Badgers often pause here to scratch and groom their fur. They moult during the summer.

Notice the scratch marks on the tree trunk. The Badgers have made these with their claws.

Torn-up tufts of grass are a sign that a Badger has been trying to get at an insect at the grass roots. Patches of flattened undergrowth show where Badgers play.

Badgers eat earthworms, Rabbits, fruit, small rodents and wasp nests. The remains of wasp and bee nests are left spread out on the ground like this.

If you follow a Badger path out of a wood and into a field, you may find Badger hairs caught on barbed wire.

If a path near the sett leads under low branches or fallen trees, it is a Badger run. It may lead to a stream or to another sett entrance.

This furrow has been made by Badgers moving soil away from the sett entrance.

Badgers rub their fur and clean their claws on trees. Look for scratch marks, dirt and hairs on tree bark.

Look for hay, bracken, dry leaves and moss near the sett. This is bedding material dropped by the Badger as it drags the foliage backwards into the sett.

The sett

Ventilation hole

Entrance

Mound of earth

Sleeping chambers

Breeding chamber

Setts can be dug as long as 20 metres and are often on more than one level with several entrances. Sometimes Badgers share the sett with Foxes. Every winter the Badgers clean out their sett.

Badgers are clean, tidy animals and always use special holes outside the sett as dung pits. The droppings can be liquid, or dry and sausage-shaped.

9

Stoats and Weasels

When you go for a country walk, you may be lucky enough to see a Stoat or a Weasel. They are mainly nocturnal, but you may see them during the day. These animals are carnivores, which means that they eat other animals. They hunt mostly by scent and hearing, rather than sight, so keep quite still if you see one—it may not notice you. Stoats and Weasels are very inquisitive and sit up on their hind legs to look around.

The other animals on these pages are closely related to Stoats and Weasels.

Spot the difference

Stoat

Weasel

IF YOU ARE NOT SURE WHETHER YOU ARE SEEING A STOAT OR A WEASEL, LOOK AT THE ANIMAL'S TAIL. A STOAT'S TAIL HAS A BLACK TIP. STOATS ARE LARGER THAN WEASELS

Tracks

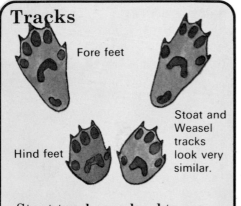

Fore feet

Hind feet

Stoat and Weasel tracks look very similar.

Stoat tracks are hard to see except in snow or very soft ground, because Stoats are so light. All the animals on these pages have five toes.

Hunting

Stoats and Weasels both attack animals larger than themselves. Rabbits are so frightened of Stoats that they become dazed. The Stoat then leaps and attacks the Rabbit with its sharp teeth. If you find a dead Rabbit with the back of the head gnawed away, you may have disturbed a Stoat at a meal.

Stoat in winter

In northern countries, like Scotland, the Stoat's fur turns white in winter, although its tail tip stays black. In its white coat, the Stoat is called an Ermine. The Ermine is well camouflaged in snow.

Weasels

Weasels are long and slender and can easily crawl down small holes or into cracks in walls or rocks. They can follow mice and voles into their burrows to catch them, and will sometimes sleep in their victim's hole after the meal. Like Stoats, Weasels hunt in family groups, called packs.

Martens

Stoats and Weasels are quite common, but if you see a marten you will be very lucky indeed. The only species in Britain is the shy Pine Marten which is now very rare and lives only in remote mountain areas. Both Pine and Beech Martens live in other parts of Europe and in Asia.

Pine Martens

Pine Martens live in or near trees, including pines. They are expert climbers and can even catch squirrels. At night they will sleep in a tree hollow, a rocky crevice or sometimes in a magpie's nest.

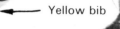

← Yellow bib

Wood Mouse

Beech Martens

As they like rocky places, Beech Martens are sometimes called Stone Martens. Their fur is greyer than the Pine Marten's and they have a white bib on their front.

To open eggs, martens bite an oblong, almost rectangular hole in the shell.

Feeding

As well as eating squirrels, mice, insects and berries, martens also raid hen-houses, bee hives and pigeon lofts for food. Beech Martens often live near farms where these things can be found. Dead birds, egg shells, Hedgehog spines and skins or droppings in a loft or shed are all signs that a Beech Marten has been there.

European Mink

Minks

Mink live near streams and marshes and swim well. They eat fishes, water birds and frogs and, like Polecats, kill far more than they need. The European Mink does not live in Britain, but wild American minks, which have escaped from fur farms, are a common pest.

Polecats

Polecats like wooded, hilly country. They are now rare in Britain. They have scent glands which smell strongly. Sometimes they store live frogs for the winter, first paralysing the frog with a bite and then pushing it into a burrow until it is needed.

Foxes

Foxes are more difficult to watch than Badgers—they travel further and change their homes more often. They live in all sorts of places, from woodland to moorland. Some now live in towns.

The best time to see Foxes is in May and June when the cubs are young and playful and when the adults still bring them food.

A Fox's home, called an earth, is often an old Rabbit burrow made larger, or a Badger sett. You can smell the Fox's musty scent around the entrance if the earth is occupied. Watch from a tree in the early morning or evening.

Tracks

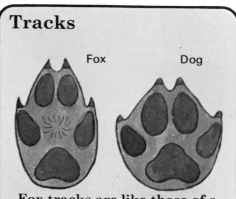

Fox tracks are like those of a dog, but the claw marks are slimmer and more pointed and there is a much wider space between the marks of the front and back pads.

Droppings

Fox droppings are sausage-shaped, with a spirally twisted point at one end. They vary in colour from black to grey depending on what the Fox has been eating.

Growing up

Foxes sometimes bury food and return to collect it later. These cubs are digging up food buried by their mother.

When the cubs are six weeks old, they play outside the earth, fighting over food the vixen brings them. Look for reddish hairs and the remains of meals. You may see bones, feathers and Rabbits' feet.

Cubs are usually born in March or April. For the first four weeks they are suckled by the female, called a vixen, in the earth. The male or dog Fox leaves food outside for her, but he does not help her care for the cubs.

Feeding

By summer the cubs are beginning to hunt alone. Their mother has taught them how to catch animals, like voles, mice, insects and squirrels, by springing into the air and pouncing.

To catch an earthworm, a Fox carefully watches to detect its exact position. Then the Fox stabs its nose downwards and grabs.

Young Foxes often hunt near Rabbit warrens, hoping to surprise a weak or sickly Rabbit. Like Stoats, Foxes may jump and somersault to attract their prey.

Foxes may scavenge in rubbish dumps, looking for bones and other scraps. Fruits, like blackberries, are also welcome food for a hungry Fox.

Under cover of night, Foxes may attack farm poultry. You may find hens, ducks or pheasants abandoned by Foxes. They usually bite the bird's head off.

Foxes will also scavenge for food in dustbins, even though this means taking the risk of approaching houses.

Winter

In winter, food is scarce and adult Foxes may protect their own food supply and territory by driving young Foxes away. Foxes mark their area, or territory, by leaving their strongly scented droppings on the ground, or on little hillocks or tree stumps.

Winter is the mating season and the time when dog Foxes establish their territory and when vixens prepare the earth for the cubs. These Foxes will have a family of their own in the spring.

Otters

Otters live by rivers and the sea. They are nocturnal and wander long distances at night. During the day they rest in their well-hidden nests, called holts. These are made in hollow trees or at the end of tunnels in river banks, sometimes with an underwater entrance.

At night Otters are easily disturbed, but quiet daytime visits to look for signs will not worry them. Wait for Otters on a bridge where they are used to seeing people. Listen for the Otter's soft clear whistle.

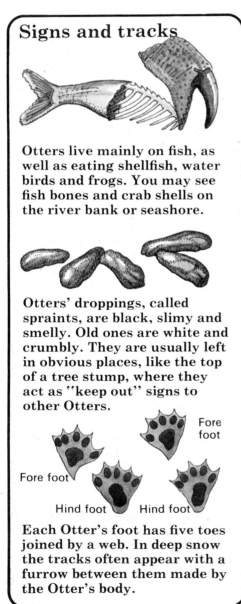

Signs and tracks

Otters live mainly on fish, as well as eating shellfish, water birds and frogs. You may see fish bones and crab shells on the river bank or seashore.

Otters' droppings, called spraints, are black, slimy and smelly. Old ones are white and crumbly. They are usually left in obvious places, like the top of a tree stump, where they act as "keep out" signs to other Otters.

Fore foot

Fore foot

Hind foot   Hind foot

Each Otter's foot has five toes joined by a web. In deep snow the tracks often appear with a furrow between them made by the Otter's body.

Look for Otter slides like this one down muddy banks into water, or in sand dunes or snow.

Otters are very playful animals. You can sometimes see them leaping in and out of the water just for fun.

Otters swim and dive well using the strong tail as a rudder and the front legs for steering and balance. Otter fur is waterproof.

The position of the eyes, ears and nose allow the Otter to breathe and look round without lifting its head too much when swimming.

A line of bubbles like this is a sign that an Otter may be swimming beneath the surface.

Cubs have to be taught to go into the water, but they immediately know how to swim. As soon as they have learnt to hunt, the male, or dog, leaves them. The female, or bitch, stays with them for some months.

Under water, the ears and nostrils close to stop water entering.

Bats

Look for bats in the evening when they hunt for insects, especially near lakes and streams and in woodland.

Bats are the only mammals that can fly. Their finger bones are very long, and skin is stretched over them to make a wing, which is attached to the hind leg. When bats fly, they spread their hind legs to keep their wings open. Most European bats also have skin that stretches between their legs, enclosing the tail. This skin can be formed into a pouch for catching flying insects.

Hunting in the dark

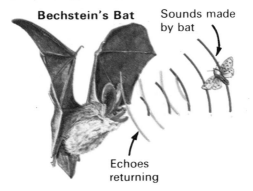

Bechstein's Bat

Sounds made by bat

Echoes returning

Bats rely on their sharp hearing to hunt in the dark. They make high-pitched noises as they fly. From the returning echoes, bats can tell the exact position of flying insects.

Roosting and hibernation

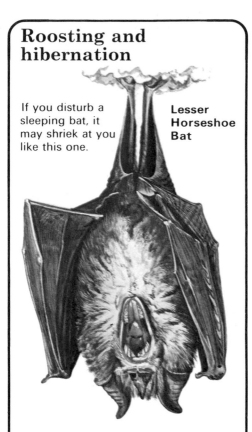

If you disturb a sleeping bat, it may shriek at you like this one.

Lesser Horseshoe Bat

Most bats sleep during the day, hanging by their claws in a quiet, dark roost. From October until March, bats hibernate. They sleep in hollow trees, caves, old mines or lofts, but they dislike dust and cobwebs and may choose quite new buildings. If you find bats hibernating, don't disturb them—they may die.

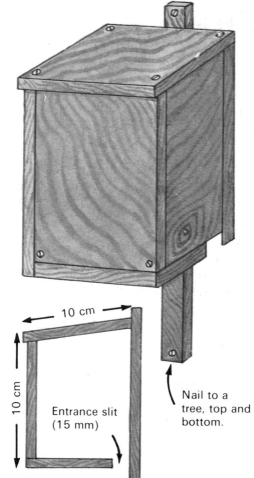

10 cm

10 cm

Entrance slit (15 mm)

Nail to a tree, top and bottom.

Making a bat box

You can attract bats to your garden with a bat box like this. Use thick, rough, untreated wood so that the bats can get a grip on the surfaces. The small entrance slit prevents squirrels or birds from moving into the box. Attach it to a tree at least 1.5 metres from the ground. You may have to try putting your box in different positions before bats use it.

Greater Horseshoe Bats

Horseshoe bats get their name from the shape of the fleshy part of the nose called the "nose-leaf". The Greater Horseshoe Bat flies very low and picks up insects from the ground as well as in the air.

Pipistrelles

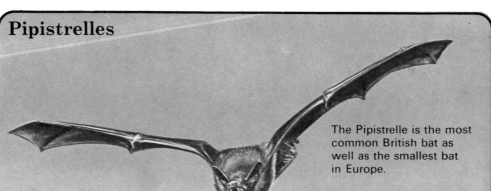

The Pipistrelle is the most common British bat as well as the smallest bat in Europe.

You may see these bats in towns, flying round street lamps, as well as in the country. Their flight is quick and jerky. However, it is almost impossible to identify a particular species of bat in flight, because they all look very similar in the dark. If you can examine one closely, its size and the shape of its face and ears will help you to identify it.

Hedgehogs, Moles and Shrews

Hedgehogs

Hedgehogs are common, and are one of the easiest mammals to watch. You are most likely to see one at night, trundling across a field or lane, or under a hedge. Look in gardens and churchyards.

Hedgehogs grunt and snuffle and sometimes squeal loudly. Listen for the loud rustling of leaves in ditches.

When frightened, a Hedgehog rolls itself into a tight ball with its prickles sticking up. Many are killed by cars, and you may find their bodies on roads. In winter, hibernating Hedgehogs often die when rubbish dumps and piles of leaves are burnt.

Strange behaviour

Hedgehogs sometimes roll on fruit and carry it away on their spines. It is possible that they do it on purpose, but this seems unlikely.

Hedgehogs climb well and can get over high fences. If they fall from a height, they land on their spines which act as a cushion so that they do not hurt themselves.

Hedgehogs hibernate from late October to March in a nest of grass, moss and leaves. They curl up like this to sleep.

Try tempting Hedgehogs to your garden each night by leaving out a saucer of bread and milk.

Moles

Moles live almost anywhere where the soil is soft enough to dig and where earthworms are plentiful. They can be found in farmland, parks and football fields, where they are a pest. Moles live alone and spend most of their time underground. They are mainly nocturnal, but they sometimes appear during the day. Look for them in spring in the breeding season when males chase one another. You may see one drinking in a ditch, or looking for earthworms after heavy rain.

Moles have soft grey-black, velvety fur which lies smoothly in any direction. The snout is pink and very sensitive. Their front legs are short and powerful with shovel-shaped feet which are used for digging. Moles hear well, but their small eyes are often hidden by fur and sometimes by skin.

All these mammals are insectivores, which means that they live mainly on insects. They also eat slugs and earthworms, and Hedgehogs will eat frogs, birds' eggs and even Adders.

They all need to eat a lot to survive and so they spend most of their time searching for food.

Baby Hedgehogs are born naked and blind. Their spines are soft at first, but when they have hardened, they are sharp. Be careful handling Hedgehogs. Fleas live on their bodies, close to the spines.

A female Hedgehog is called a sow, and the male is known as a boar.

Shrews

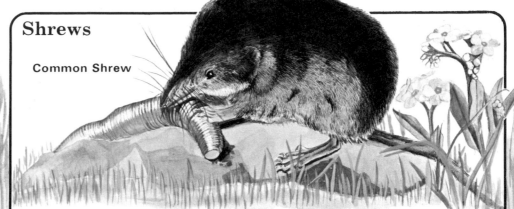

Common Shrew

Common Shrews and Pygmy Shrews live in thick undergrowth in fields, woods, hedgerows and ditches. They eat beetles, slugs and worms, above and below the ground, and some plants.

You can tell a shrew from a mouse by its long, twitching, whiskery snout.

Shrews have a musky smell and, perhaps for this reason, their bodies are rarely eaten by predators.

Water Shrews

Air bubbles caught in the fur make Water Shrews look silvery under water.

Water Shrews live along the banks of streams, rivers and lakes. Most of their day is spent sleeping or looking for food. They eat gnats, beetles, snails, worms and small fishes.

Water Shrews swim well and if you disturb one you will hear the splash as it jumps into the water.

Molehill   Fortress

Nest

The fortress may have a larder where worms are stored.

Exit tunnels lead to the surface at an angle.

A sure sign of Moles is a series of small heaps of earth called molehills. These are made by Moles pushing surplus soil out from their burrows. If the earth is fresh, the molehill is new. Older ones have grass growing on them.

An extra-large molehill is called a fortress. Inside is a nest for sleeping lined with dead leaves, moss and grass. A smaller fortress is used for breeding.

Burrows are so narrow that a Mole's fur is squeezed clean as it travels through. Hunting burrows are deeper.

Rats, Mice and Voles

Common Rats and House Mice live in colonies in all sorts of places close to people. Look for signs of them in warehouses, barns, rubbish dumps, haystacks, by canals, in offices and homes. They breed very fast, eat almost anything, do great damage and spread disease.

House Mice have been known to survive in cold stores by feeding on frozen food. These mice grow special thick coats to keep themselves warm.

Rats, mice and voles are all rodents. Their teeth are specially adapted for gnawing.

Ship Rats

Tail is longer than Common Rat's.

Large ears

Ship Rats are so called because they are usually found on ships or in dock areas. They are also called Black Rats, though not all of them are black. They are very good at climbing.

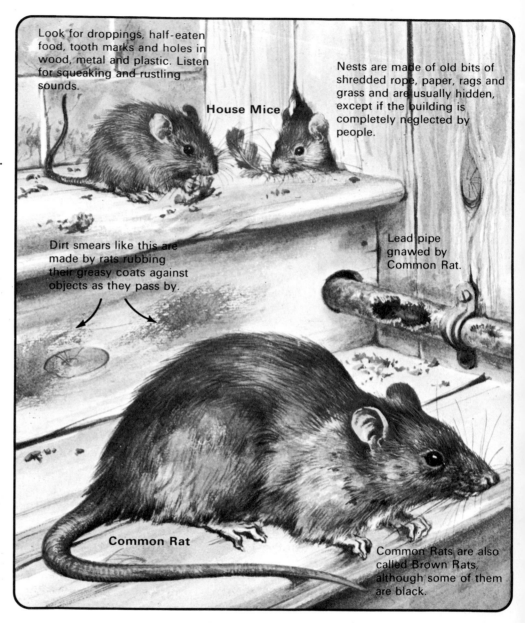

Look for droppings, half-eaten food, tooth marks and holes in wood, metal and plastic. Listen for squeaking and rustling sounds.

House Mice

Nests are made of old bits of shredded rope, paper, rags and grass and are usually hidden, except if the building is completely neglected by people.

Dirt smears like this are made by rats rubbing their greasy coats against objects as they pass by.

Lead pipe gnawed by Common Rat.

Common Rat

Common Rats are also called Brown Rats, although some of them are black.

Harvest Mice

Harvest Mice are the smallest mice in Europe. They live in fields, reed beds and tall grasses. They use their tails as an extra limb when climbing.

Wood Mice

Wood Mice, or Field Mice, are common in the country. You may find their stores of nuts and seeds hidden in old birds' nests, nest boxes and cracks in walls or tree stumps.

Voles

You can tell voles from rats and mice by their blunter faces, small ears and short tails. They are mainly nocturnal and move quickly. Voles are common although they are eaten by many meat-eating animals, such as Foxes and birds of prey.

If you look in undergrowth, you may find vole runs, which will probably lead to burrows. Look for gnawed roots and other feeding signs. Voles damage trees by gnawing bark too—look for their fine tooth marks.

Bank Voles

Long tail

Look in banks and ditches bordering lanes and woods. Bank Voles eat grasses, nuts, buds, shoots, berries and seeds. They are good at swimming and also climb well and will gnaw bark high up in trees.

Field Voles

Short tail

Field Voles live in grassland, heath, dunes and woods. They eat grasses, rushes, bark and clover.

In winter, they make runs under snow, lining them with grass. You can see these tunnels when snow has melted.

Water Voles attack crops like turnips from below. They eat the whole turnip before starting on the next one.

Water Voles swim with only their noses showing above the water.

Broken bits of plant are piled up ready to eat.

Water Voles

Water Voles live on the edges of streams, small ponds and canals. Approach quietly and you may see one on the bank grooming its fur. If frightened, it will dive into the water and may stay under for over 30 seconds before it comes up in the safety of a tunnel in the bank, or perhaps behind a water lily or some rushes. Look for the tunnels in banks close to the water's edge.

Feeding signs

Mice, voles, rats and squirrels eat a variety of nuts and cones. Here are some typical signs of handling.

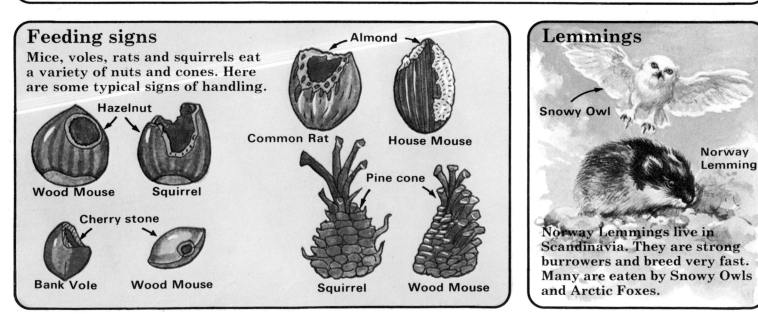

Almond

Hazelnut

Wood Mouse

Squirrel

Common Rat

House Mouse

Cherry stone

Bank Vole

Wood Mouse

Pine cone

Squirrel

Wood Mouse

Lemmings

Snowy Owl

Norway Lemming

Norway Lemmings live in Scandinavia. They are strong burrowers and breed very fast. Many are eaten by Snowy Owls and Arctic Foxes.

19

Squirrels and Dormice

Red Squirrels

Most Red Squirrels live in forests of coniferous trees, like pine and fir, in remote areas. If you find any of the signs shown on the opposite page, leave pieces of chocolate, nuts or raisins nearby (perhaps on a tree stump) and settle into a comfortable hiding place to wait. Early morning is a good time.

Although squirrels will dart away if you disturb them, they will often come back to have another look at you. Keep still and you may see an excited squirrel chattering at you from a safe place in the tree above.

Grey Squirrels

Grey Squirrels were introduced to Britain from North America and are now more common here than Red Squirrels. They live in city parks and gardens as well as in woodland. When food is scarce in winter, they will sometimes eat out of your hand, but be careful—they may bite.

Squirrels have very good eyesight and hearing. They are always twitching their noses and whiskers, ready to sense danger.

Unlike most animals, squirrels can use their forepaws as hands.

The big bushy tail helps the squirrel to balance as it runs along branches and jumps from tree to tree.

Red Squirrels moult their fur twice a year. The softer, longer winter coat keeps them warm in winter.

Squirrels can leap as far as five metres or more between branches.

Baby squirrels are born between April and June and are blind and naked at birth. After seven or eight weeks, they climb out of the drey and begin exploring the tree tops. Use binoculars to watch them closely.

Nests called dreys are about the size of a football. Look in forks of trees and in hollows. They are made of twigs, but the inside may be lined with moss, leaves, fur and feathers. In bad weather squirrels will stay in the drey all day, but they do not hibernate.

Three vertical, parallel scratch marks on bark are made by the squirrel's longest fingers and toes. To see them, you may have to climb the tree. They are usually on the route to the drey.

Squirrels eat seeds, buds, fungi, cones and fruits. They often have a favourite feeding place, such as a tree stump, and they scatter food remains around it.

Squirrels pull off strips of bark to get at the layer beneath.

Sometimes they gnaw away a ring of bark at the base of the tree.

Every autumn, squirrels bury or hide food. Some of it is eaten during the winter, but most is forgotten and lost.

Squirrel tracks nearly always start and end at a tree, and the feet are usually turned out a little.

Droppings are hard to find except in snow.

Dormice

Common Dormouse

Dormice live in woods and scrub. Look for their round summer nests, made of grass and leaves, in creepers. They sometimes use old birds' nests or even nesting boxes.

Edible Dormouse

This large dormouse looks like a squirrel and lives in woods and gardens. It gets very fat before winter hibernation.

Deer

In Britain, deer herds are most common in the Scottish highlands and in woodland parks belonging to country estates.

Deer are shy of strange objects, so hide in a tree or behind a wall or rock to watch them. You can also watch from a parked car. The best times are at dawn and dusk. Always face the wind as deer have a strong sense of smell.

During the rutting or breeding season (usually in the autumn), some deer can be bad-tempered. Approach them with care.

The picture shows you some of the different kinds of deer you may see in Britain and the signs to look for. You will not see all the signs at the same time of year.

Red Deer

The roaring or "belling" of a male Red Deer is very loud. Listen for it at dawn and dusk in the rutting season (Sept–Oct). At this time, the males, or stags, often wallow in mud or peat. A little later, the colour of the coat changes from dark red to brownish grey for the winter months.

In October, the Fallow buck marks out a rutting territory. He tears bushes with his antlers, scrapes the ground with his hooves and marks the area with scent from glands under his eyes. The does visit him here.

Roe Deer kids

Roe Deer kids are born in May or June. This one is about two weeks old. Twins are common and they stay with the doe for up to a year. When alarmed, a kid will crouch down on the ground. Its spotted coat matches its background and makes it difficult for enemies to spot.

Baby Red Deer are called calves, and baby Fallow Deer are known as fawns.

Red Deer

Red Deer tear down twigs and buds from trees up to two metres from the ground. This is a female, called a hind.

Fallow Deer

While they grow, a deer's antlers are covered with a furry coat called velvet. When growth stops, the velvet begins to strip off. This Sika Deer is helping the process by rubbing (or fraying) its antlers against a young tree. Look for scraped off velvet and marks on tree trunks.

Sika Deer

Deer have no fixed homes, but they do rest in temporary lairs. Look for flattened vegetation and loose leaves, or twigs that have been scraped away.

Roe Deer

Roe rings like this were once called fairy rings. They are made by a male Roe Deer, called a buck, chasing a female, called a doe, in a circle. They do this during the Roe Deers' rutting season in July and August.

Antlers

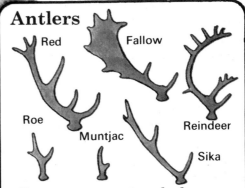

Every year, most male deer grow and shed (or cast) a pair of antlers. Look for cast, gnawed antlers (usually found singly). The larger the antlers, the older the deer.

Signs

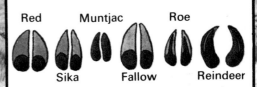

Deer have cloven (divided) hooves formed from two toes. Reindeer hooves are very broad and deeply cleft, splaying out to support them in snow.

Look for twigs and shoots that have been torn or broken off, gnawed vegetables and bark stripped off trees. These can all be signs of deer.

Deer droppings, called fewmets, are dark brown or black. Look for large piles of them close to feeding places.

23

Rabbits

You can see Rabbits in almost every type of countryside, especially on commons, sand dunes and in woodland. Rabbits live together in groups of burrows called warrens. They usually come out at dawn and dusk, but you may see them at any time.

Rabbit populations increase very quickly. Each female (called a doe) has an average of ten babies each year. The young become adults within three or four months and they then begin to breed themselves.

Rabbit droppings are left in piles on mole hills and small banks around the warren. The same places are used regularly. The droppings are yellowy brown at first and become paler with age.

Rabbits use their forepaws to dig their burrows. They push the soil out behind them with their hind paws.

This is the breeding burrow of a young doe. She covers the entrance with earth when she leaves the stop to protect the young from intruders.

Well-worn paths on the surface connect the burrow entrances.

The young are born in a nest of hay and their mother's fur in a special breeding burrow called a stop. They are naked, blind and helpless at birth.

Strong does dig their stops off tunnels in the main warren; younger does choose a different site away from the other burrows.

Rabbits spend a lot of time resting and sleeping in their burrows.

Rabbits are eaten by birds of prey, Foxes, Stoats and Weasels. They can only defend themselves by kicking with their strong hind legs, but usually they run away.

Buzzard

Male rabbits, called bucks, moult between July and September. Look for their hairs caught in hedges and fences.

If alarmed or curious, Rabbits sit up and look around, moving their ears to pick up every sound. When really frightened, they thump their hind feet on the ground and raise their white tails to warn others. Then they bolt for the nearest hole.

Rabbits are sometimes called "landscape gardeners" because the plants they like to eat disappear from the area round the warren. New plants, which Rabbits don't like, grow in their place.

This Rabbit is grooming its fur. Rabbits use their front paws and tongues to keep their fur clean.

Spot the difference

4 cm

Rabbit

Brown Hare

6 cm

Although Rabbits and Hares look a bit alike, they are easy to tell apart. Hares are bigger, have longer ears with black tips, longer hind legs and are usually solitary. Their tracks are larger too.

Food

Grasses

Corn

Trees

Vegetables

Rabbits eat grasses, corn crops, root vegetables and young trees. Look for marks of grazing on crops along the edges of fields, and for damage to plants in nurseries and gardens.

Rabbits feed on trees up to 60 cm from the ground. Look for nibbled bark and tooth marks on branches, buds and fruits.

Hares

Look for Brown Hares on farmland, moors, dunes and in woodland. They feed mostly at night and live alone, except during the breeding season. You may see a female, called a doe, resting in her form. The form is a hiding place hollowed out of soft grass where the Hare spends the day resting. She will dash away if you come close, zigzagging to put you off her trail.

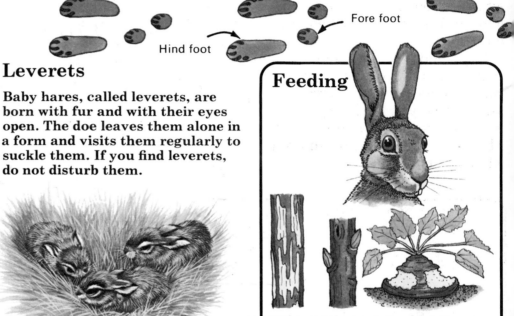

The fore feet touch the ground first. Then the hind feet land just in front of the fore feet.

Tracks

The soles of a hare's feet are covered with hairs, so tracks are difficult to see on a firm surface although the claws leave a mark.

A hare's trail is easy to identify in snow or on soft ground. You can tell how fast the hare was moving by the spacing of the tracks.

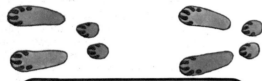

Hind foot

Fore foot

Mad March Hares

In February and March, hares gather to mate. Males leap and kick, chase in circles and box each other.

Leverets

Baby hares, called leverets, are born with fur and with their eyes open. The doe leaves them alone in a form and visits them regularly to suckle them. If you find leverets, do not disturb them.

Feeding

Hares live mainly on grasses, but they also damage fruit trees and vegetables, particularly in winter. Look for the marks of their sharp, curved front teeth in chewed swedes and turnips and on tree bark. They also bite shoots from young trees.

Droppings

Hares' droppings look like those of Rabbits, but they are larger and a bit flattened. They are yellow brown and quite dry. You can see the plant matter that the hare has eaten.

Blue Hares

Summer coat

The Blue or Mountain Hare lives in the north and in Ireland. It is smaller than the Brown Hare and its ears are not so long. In winter, the Blue Hare's fur becomes white or blue-grey to camouflage it against snow. It shelters between rocks or in a small burrow.

Winter coat

Seals

Seals are sea animals, although they sometimes swim up rivers. Every year they gather on quiet, remote shores like those of the Faroe Islands, the Hebrides and off Ireland and South Wales to breed.

There are two kinds which are common round our coasts —the Grey Seal which breeds in autumn and usually chooses a rocky coast with caves and cliffs for its rookery (breeding place), and the Common Seal which breeds in June and July and prefers sandy beaches and flat rocks.

Find a comfortable place in some rocks and watch from there. Seals are inquisitive animals, so you could try playing a mouth organ to them. They may come over to find out what's happening!

You can tell bull seals (males) from cows (females) by their larger size.

Look out for heads bobbing in the water. Seals sometimes sleep in the water.

Grey Seal pups are born with white fur, which they moult after about three weeks. This pup's fur is stained brown with seaweed.

Grey Seals

Grey Seals rarely have twins. If you see a cow with two pups, she is probably acting as a foster mother to one of them.

Young seals are not always good tempered. Don't give them a chance to bite you.

Common Seals

Although Grey Seals' flippers look tiny, they have claws with a hook-like grip. They use these to pull themselves up steep rocky slopes.

It is hard to tell the difference between Grey and Common Seals at a distance. Common Seals are usually smaller and slighter, and spend less time in the water.

Seals basking in sunshine usually keep a clear space between themselves and their neighbours.

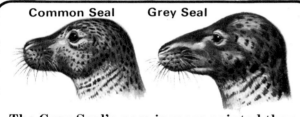

Common Seal   Grey Seal

The Grey Seal's nose is more pointed than the Common Seal's.

How a seal moves

Seals are excellent swimmers, but they move in clumsy jerks on land. Their hind flippers only stretch backwards and cannot push. Watch them closely to see how, despite this, they manage to move around.

Moving quickly

Moving slowly

Mark of hind flippers

Mark of fore claw

Mark of fore claw

Direction of movement

1
Fore flipper moved forward and claws dug in sand.

2
Hind part of body arched and drawn forward.

3
Front of body raised on flippers and pushed forward by hind end.

More mammals to spot

Meat-eaters

Wild Cat. Thick woods and rocky mountains in Europe, including Scotland. Body 64 cm. Tail 31 cm.

Fore foot

Lynx. Woods on rocky mountainous ground. Not in Britain. Remote parts of Europe. Body 1.5 m. Tail 17 cm.

Fore foot

Pine Marten. Remote woods. Britain's rarest mammal, as many were trapped for fur. Body 47 cm. Tail 24 cm.

Hind foot

Fore foot

Beech Marten. Rocky parts of Europe, often near farms. Not in Britain. Body 45 cm. Tail 24 cm.

Wolf. Woods and mountains in Italy and Norway. Not in Britain. Body 1.2 m. Tail 35 cm.

Hind foot

Bats

Natterer's Bat. Mostly woodland, but also towns. Slow, steady flight. Common in Britain. Body 4.5 cm. Tail 3.5 cm. Arm 3.5 cm.

Daubenton's or Water Bat. Colonies near water. Flies low and fast. Body 4.5 cm. Tail 3.5 cm. Arm 3.5 cm.

Long-eared Bat. Body 4.5 cm. Tail 3.7 cm. Arm 3.7 cm.

Ferret. Tame white Polecat used to hunt rabbits. Some escape and live wild. The descendants of these are often brown and look like wild Polecats. Same size as Polecat.

Polecat. Woods and scrub in Europe. Rare in Britain. Body 38 cm. Tail 24 cm.

Hind foot   Fore foot

Winter

Summer

Fore foot of Arctic Fox

Fore foot of Fox

Arctic Fox. Arctic tundra. Coat changes from brown to white in winter. Body 57 cm. Tail 30 cm.

Brown Bear. Mountains and forests in parts of Europe. Not in Britain. Hibernates. Body 2 m. Tail 10 cm.

Bear's hind foot

Bear's fore foot

Fox. Near woodland or scrub. Common in Britain and found all over Europe. Body 68 cm. Tail 40 cm.

Noctule. Woods and parks. Flies high. Body 7.5 cm. Tail 5 cm. Arm 5 cm.

Whiskered Bat. Near trees. Body 5 cm. Tail 4.5 cm. Arm 3.5 cm.

Blue Hare. Moors and woods. Scotland and Ireland. Scottish hare is partly white in winter. Body 50 cm. Tail 6 cm.

Brown Hare. Farmland and moors. May be more grey in winter. Body 58 cm. Tail 9 cm.

Hind foot   Fore foot

Hind foot   Fore foot

Rabbit. Common in woods, moors, dunes, grassland. Body 40 cm. Tail 6 cm.

Hind foot   Fore foot

29

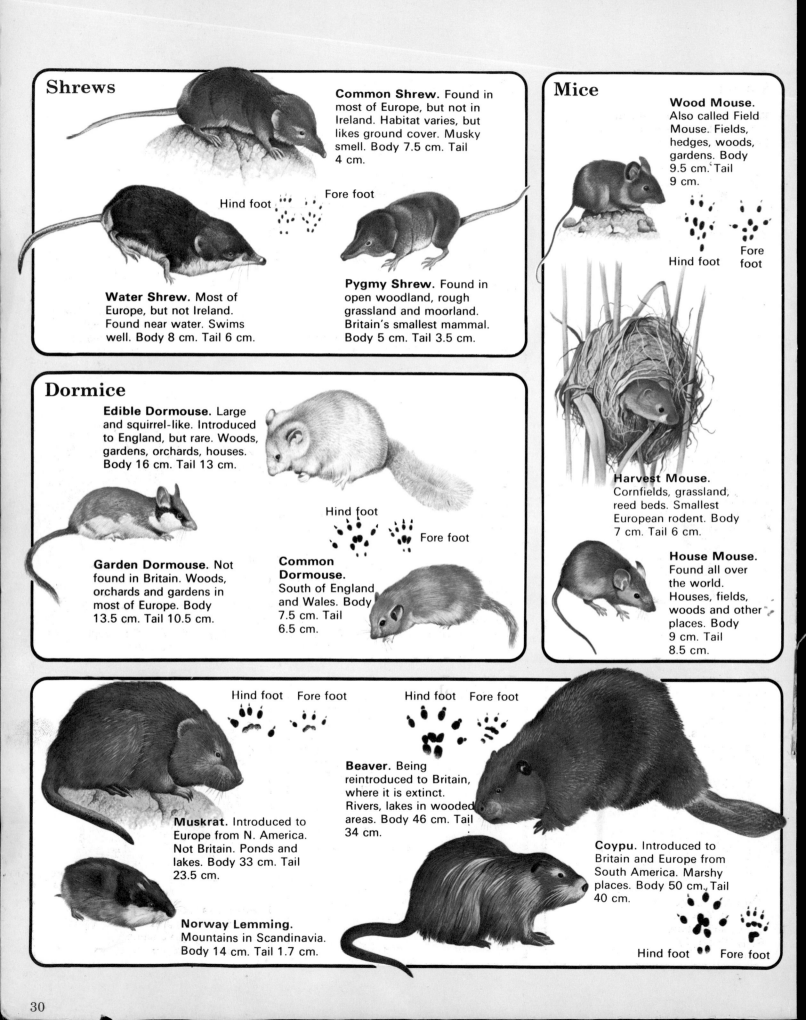

Shrews

Common Shrew. Found in most of Europe, but not in Ireland. Habitat varies, but likes ground cover. Musky smell. Body 7.5 cm. Tail 4 cm.

Hind foot   Fore foot

Water Shrew. Most of Europe, but not Ireland. Found near water. Swims well. Body 8 cm. Tail 6 cm.

Pygmy Shrew. Found in open woodland, rough grassland and moorland. Britain's smallest mammal. Body 5 cm. Tail 3.5 cm.

Mice

Wood Mouse. Also called Field Mouse. Fields, hedges, woods, gardens. Body 9.5 cm. Tail 9 cm.

Hind foot   Fore foot

Harvest Mouse. Cornfields, grassland, reed beds. Smallest European rodent. Body 7 cm. Tail 6 cm.

House Mouse. Found all over the world. Houses, fields, woods and other places. Body 9 cm. Tail 8.5 cm.

Dormice

Edible Dormouse. Large and squirrel-like. Introduced to England, but rare. Woods, gardens, orchards, houses. Body 16 cm. Tail 13 cm.

Hind foot   Fore foot

Garden Dormouse. Not found in Britain. Woods, orchards and gardens in most of Europe. Body 13.5 cm. Tail 10.5 cm.

Common Dormouse. South of England and Wales. Body 7.5 cm. Tail 6.5 cm.

Hind foot   Fore foot   Hind foot   Fore foot

Muskrat. Introduced to Europe from N. America. Not Britain. Ponds and lakes. Body 33 cm. Tail 23.5 cm.

Beaver. Being reintroduced to Britain, where it is extinct. Rivers, lakes in wooded areas. Body 46 cm. Tail 34 cm.

Coypu. Introduced to Britain and Europe from South America. Marshy places. Body 50 cm. Tail 40 cm.

Norway Lemming. Mountains in Scandinavia. Body 14 cm. Tail 1.7 cm.

Hind foot   Fore foot

Voles

Water Vole. In or near slow-flowing rivers and lakes. Also grasslands. Body 19 cm. Tail 12 cm.

Hind foot   Fore foot

Bank Vole. Banks, hedgerows, woods, scrub. Body 10 cm. Tail 5.5 cm.

Field Vole. Also called Short-tailed Vole. Damp pastures, open woodland. Body 11.5 cm. Tail 3.5 cm.

Hoofed animals

Both male and female Reindeer have antlers.

Fore foot

Elk. USSR and Scandinavia. Not in Britain. 2 m high at shoulder.

Fore foot

Reindeer. North Europe and introduced to Cairngorms in Scotland. 1 m high at shoulder.

Ibex. Wild goat. High rocky mountains in Alps, Spain and Norway. Not in Britain. 75 cm high at shoulder.

Chamois. Alps and Pyrenees. Not in Britain. Wooded and rocky mountains. 75 cm high at shoulder.

Fore foot

Mouflon. Wild sheep. Mountains in Europe. Not in Britain. 70 cm high at shoulder.

Fore foot

Common Rat. Near people, and woods, banks. Body 24 cm. Tail 20 cm.

Hind foot

Fore foot

Ship Rat. Large ears, long tail. Towns, docks, ships, trees. Body 20 cm. Tail 21 cm.

Squirrels

Grey Squirrel. Common in Britain. Not in other parts of Europe. Body 27 cm. Tail 23 cm.

Fore foot   Hind foot

Red Squirrel. Mixed woodland in Europe. Body 24 cm. Tail 23 cm.

Wild Boar. Widespread in woods in Europe. Not in Britain. Young are striped. 90 cm high at shoulder.

Fore foot

Index

Glossary

The females, males and young of many British mammals have different names as do their homes and droppings. It is useful to know some of the more common ones if you study mammals.

Badger. Female: sow, Male: boar, Young: cub, Home: sett

Deer. Home: lair, Droppings: fewmets
　Fallow. Female: doe, Male: buck, Young: fawn
　Red. Female: hind, Male: stag, Young: calf
　Roe: Female: doe, Male: buck, Young: kid
Fox. Female: vixen, Male: dog, Young: cub, Home: earth
Hare. Female: doe, Male: buck, Young: leveret, Home: form

Hedgehog. Female: sow, Male: boar, Young: piglet
Marten. See **Stoat**
Mole. Breeding burrow: fortress
Mouse. Female: doe, Male: buck, Home: nest
Otter. Female: bitch, Male: dog, Young: cub, Home: holt, Droppings: spraints
Polecat. Female: jill, Male: hob, Young: kitten

Rabbit. Female: doe, Male: buck, Home: warren, Breeding burrow: stop
Rat. See **Mouse**
Seal. Female: cow, Male: bull, Young: pup, Breeding place: rookery
Squirrel. Home: drey
Stoat. Female: bitch, Male: dog, Young: kitten, Home: den
Weasel. See **Stoat**

Books to read

Collins Guide to Animal Tracks and Signs. P. Bang and P. Dahlstrom (Collins)
The Clue Book of Tracks and Signs. G. Allen and J. Denslow (Oxford)
Finding and identifying mammals in Britain. G. B. Corbet (British Museum (Natural History))
Mammals of Britain. Their Tracks, Trails and Signs. M. J. Lawrence and R. W. Brown (Blandford)
Mammals. C. König (Collins)
A Field Guide to the Mammals of Britain and Europe. F. H. van den Brink (Collins)
Mammals in Britain and Ireland. T. Jennings (A & C Black)
Foxes, Squirrels, Bats and other titles. Young Naturalist Books (Priory Press)

Badgers. E. Neal (Blandford)
Deer. R. E. Chaplin (Blandford)
Mammals of Great Britain. N. Duerden. (Jarrold paperback)
The Handbook of British Mammals. ed. H. N. Southern and G. B. Corbet (Blackwell)
You can borrow these books from your public library.

Clubs and societies

The Council for Nature (address: The Zoological Society, Regent's Park, London NW1) is a representative body of more than 450 societies, and will supply the addresses of your local **Natural History Societies.** (Send a stamped self-addressed envelope for the list.) Many of these have specialist sections, and almost all have field meetings. The Council will also give you the address of your local **County Naturalist Trust** which may have a junior branch. Many of the Trusts have meetings and lectures and offer opportunities for work on nature reserves.

If you are interested in local field work and in making surveys of the mammals in your area, join the **Mammal Society.** Write to Ms Lenton (address: 5 St Stephens Court, Bath, Avon) for information about the Youth Membership.

The **RSPCA** organizes field courses and lectures on wildlife and natural history. Write to the Education Department, RSPCA, Causeway, Horsham, Sussex.

Your local museum may have a section on mammals where you can find out more about them.

PRINTED IN BELGIUM